PHOTOGRAPHIC CREDITS

© ALL ACTION

© LONDON FEATURES INTERNATIONAL LTD

© REDFERNS

Copyright © 1997 UFO MUSIC LTD

All rights reserved. Printed in Great Britain. No part of this book may be used or reproduced in any manner whatsoever without written permission except in the case of brief quotations embodied in critical articles or reviews.

UFO Music Ltd 18 Hanway Street London W1P 9DD England
Telephone: 0171 636 1281   Fax: 0171 636 0738

First published in Great Britain 1997
UFO Music Ltd 18 Hanway Street
London W1P 9DD

The author and publishers have made every effort to contact all copyright holders. Any who for any reason have not been contacted are invited to write to the publishers so that a full acknowledgment may be made in subsequent editions of this work.

ISBN 1-873884-86-9

Designed by UFO Music Ltd

the chemical brothers *life is sweet*

BY BEN WILLMOTT

Introduction

It's hard to imagine a band like The Chemical Brothers emerging from anywhere other than Manchester. They may have made their name cutting records for hip London label Junior Boys Own and become the toast of the capital's music biz glitteratti by spinning at Heavenly's Sunday Social, a weekly bash held in the sweaty basement of a Central London pub, but musically, spiritually, they are children of the vastly influential watershed scene that Manchester spawned at the turn of the 90s.

By the time Tom Rowlands and Ed Simons moved to Manchester, the city was coming to the boil. The Stone Roses had released their historic eponymous debut LP and, after facing initial indifference (the NME gave it a mere six out of ten in a modest downpage review) were well on the way to becoming the biggest new band in Britain.

Widely acknowleged to be the first so-called 'indie' shows to feature cutting edge acid house DJs alongside live acts, these shows were beery, decadent celebrations in themselves that, mainly due to the crowd's fiercely regionalist almost gang mentality, resembled the free-for-all

hedonism of clubland rather than the static, one dimensional atmosphere of traditional rock concerts.

Another vitally important factor was coming into play too. An entirely new synthesised drug, Ecstasy or MDMA, had started to surface in British clubs and was turning the fabric of Britain's youth culture inside out. Ecstasy encouraged and enabled those who took it to literally dance until sunrise without tiring. Many who took it reported that it gave them a peaceful, brimming sense of euphoria which made them feel affectionate or "loved up" towards their fellow clubbers. Football fans began taking Es on the terraces instead of drinking and cases of hooliganism dropped overnight. It felt like a revolution was about to happen.

And yet, without the waves of new electronic music reaching British shores in 1989, E culture would have been nowhere. House music, in all its various forms from acid house to techno, went so perfectly with E that they could easily have been designed for each other. E heads seemed to connect with the throbbing repetition of house, which had spread slowly but steadily from its Chicago base in the mid 80s. The very experience of clubbing, too, with its seamlessly mixed music provided by DJs often tucked away from view, placed its emphasis on clubgoers rather than stars and, again, was beautifully in tune with the effects of E.

Midway through 1989, Manchester's clubs were the best the nation had. They'd always been strong, but they had the added advantage of discovering house music before London's nighteries, which were still stuck in the death throes of the hopelessly trendy jazz-funk of the rare groove scene. The Hacienda, owned by Manc heroes and early electronic innovators New Order, was, indeed, the first in the country to let DJs like Jon Da Silva, Mike Pickering, Graeme Park and Laurent Garnier spin the obscure new 'acid' house grooves they'd rooted out on trips to the States.

Tom Rowlands had travelled up to Manchester from his native Henley-On-Thames for nights out at the Hacienda before he arrived to study in Manchester. Like many others - Manchester's University and Poly were both deluged with applications as a result of the press interest in the city's music scene -

he'd grasped that the city's nightlife made it the only place to move to. Ed Simons, meanwhile, originally from Oxford but then living in Herne Hill, South London, fancied the look of the university library and signed up for the same course, studying History at Manchester Polytechnic. Their lives would never be the same.

CHAPTER ONE

Raising the Dust

Just as Madchester, with its blend of rock's psychedelia and dance's primal beats, celebrated the fusion of disparate elements, it was such open minded eclecticism that truly gave birth to Tom and Ed's partnership.

In between lectures and later, long vinyl spinning sessions that stretched through the night, the pair bonded over any number of musical common points. Acid house, of course, was a central anchor in their mutual taste, but they also loved anarchic backcombed noiseniks The Jesus and Mary Chain. Early cut and paste sample wizards Coldcut were heroes of theirs from the start, but so were electro kings Mantronix and the Mondays, Renegade Soundwave and rappers like the Beastie Boys and Public Enemy. In 1989, the crossover between indie and dance music was still in its formative stages, but Ed and Tom had already rejected the petty cultural barriers that separate pop music's infinitely numerous tribes.

"I like all types of music," Ed told Mixmag in December 1995, "that's what it's about. there's no division. I used to like The Jesus and Mary Chain and Public Enemy at the same time." And when they weren't locked away in their bedrooms digesting each other's already mushrooming record collections, the pair were out, getting to grips with the plethora of

sounds, tastes and feelings suddenly on offer to them. They became regulars at the Hacienda and quickly became faces on the Manchester scene, pestering DJs for track titles and making alliances that would stand them in good stead for many years to come.

In 1990, they befriended fast rising Manc DJ Justin Robertson, who then worked alongside the Stone Roses' resident dancer Cressa, in Manchester's most important record shop Eastern Bloc. Situated on the ground floor of Afflecks Palace, a four-storey supermarket of second hand clothes, posters and, of course, records. If Manchester was world capital of youth culture at the start of the 90s, then Afflecks was its Buckingham Palace and Eastern Bloc its front door.

By now, with the Roses officially the world's biggest news and the Mondays not far behind, the world's media was desperate for any piece of Manchester action it could get its hands on. Bedroom-bound techno producers and local baggy hopefuls alike were driven on to knock out their own productions, press them up on white labels and cart a boxload down to Eastern Bloc, where they would inevitably fly off the shelves. DIY culture was on the rise again for the first time since the punk explosion inspired the original independent labels to strike out against the domination of the majors.

Robertson, who'd already had some success as a 'balaeric' jock known as much for his daring variety as his style, switching the pair onto little known gems and delving under the counter to produce the obscure and promos. He also ran two clubs over the next couple of years, Most Excellent and Spice, that would be instrumental in shaping Tom and Ed's musical pedigree and experience. Legend has it that the pair soon became resident "club pests" at Robertson's Most Excellent and Spice nights; tales of them swinging from the rafters, stage diving from the balcony and causing general mayhem are already legion.

"Spice and Most Excellent were about variety," Justin told The Face in February 1996, **"When house became so big that it moved to larger venues it lost its intimacy. The 'eclectic' nights sprung out of the tradition for playing chunky hip hop stuff at the end of the night. Those were the records people went the maddest to."**

DJing was the next, logical step in their partnership. Legend has it that Ed and Tom first joined forces behind the decks at a drunken wedding reception in Manchester sometime in 1990. When the invitations to play started to increase - university life is never short of opportunities for the willing DJs with decks and extensive record collections to boot - they started using the moniker Blood. That was soon jettisoned in favour of The Dust Brothers, unashamedly nicked from the American backroom boys responsible for producing the Beastie Boys' classic 'Paul's Boutique' LP, and later, Beck's much lauded 'Odelay!' album. The fact the name was stolen didn't matter to them; it sounded good and they never imagined they'd progress beyond the inebriated knees ups and dodgy backroom sessions they soundtracked that year.

the
chemical brothers

But 1990 had other delights in store for Tom and Ed. The indie-dance band Tom had formed at school was starting to gather interest. Their first single, 'Sea Of Beats,' had been pressed up by a friend of Tom's, Phil Brown. He'd intended to simply sell it directly onto shops from the boot of his car, but it was soon picked up by Eastern Bloc, with a further pair of singles and handfuls of live gigs following soon after. Ironically, it was Ariel's initial success that gave Tom and Ed their first openings as a duo, before they'd even thought of making records.

"I loved the thing of being a friend of someone in a band," Ed told Select recently, "It was exciting, bombing down to London with them."

And when Ariel signed to deConstruction, they took to the inevitable round of record industry parties. This meant capitalising on the contacts they'd made in Manchester and forging friendships with fresh allies who would prove useful sooner than they could possibly dream. Tom remembers the thrill of spotting Primal Scream's Bobby Gillespie and Kylie Minogue at a party thrown in a sumptuous country manor by trendy dance label Boy's Own. Before long, he'd be signed to the label and well on the way to remixing the Scream.

The first step was a club. But it wasn't until 1991, when university mates Phil Self and Alex Kholer offered to sort out technicalities and leave the spinning to the Brothers, that things started to happen.

Over the next year, the sleazily named Naked Under Leather inhabited all manner of run down venues either above or below pubs across Manchester. By all accounts it was an intense event. Advertised with flyers featuring a crudely drawn picture of a crotch in leather trousers, its capacity rarely exceeded a crammed-in 100 punters, more often legless on Carlsberg Special Brew than buzzing on narcotics. Smoke poured consistently onto the dancefloor throughout the night, air raid sirens sounded almost non-stop and strobes pulsed away continuously, ensuring all grip on reality was lost and making total surrender to the music the only means of survival. The Brothers, DJing as a pair, would mix up the Mondays with The Beatles, funk and Mantronix with the fearsome sounds of early European techno producers like CJ Bolland, who'd taken the softer, more soulful strains of Detroit techno and battered them into something much more sinister.

"You could see the fun to be had out of music," said Ed of the club, "more than just sitting in a club, drunk, thinking 'This is OK. We thought there was better stuff you could play. We'd really hunt hard for records - the second mix on the b-side of some house thing, then into this breakbeat of some instrumental hip hop track. It was quite like the Heavenly Social - a room full of 100 people out of their minds on beer."

Justin Robertson kept feeding the pair the very latest vinyl that arrived at Eastern Bloc and the pair would also embark on legendary searches to hunt down a record they'd heard or been tipped off about. But even then it wasn't enough.

Eventually the quest to find that elusive, definitive Naked Under Leather anthem ended - with the pair realising they were going to have to make it themselves. So they holed up in Tom's bedroom midway through 1992 and employed an ultra spartan array of equipment - one S1000 sampler, a home computer, one low rent keyboard and a £100 Hitachi hi-fi - to make 'Song To The Siren,' their first official outing as the Dust Brothers.

It was a pure distillation of the club's rampant, ramraiding sound. Stealing snatches of This Mortal Coil's 'Song To The Siren' and adding skyscraper sized drums, an apocalyptic siren and throbbing bass, the Brothers concocted their trademark sound that would shape their every release. Ed borrowed the money to press up 500 copies from a friend (who argued for 10% of all future earnings then relented - bad move) and began mining their rich seam of contacts for support. It wasn't long coming.

CHAPTER TWO

Siren Song

Ed tells a story about returning to Henley to visit his mum, arriving home to find she'd been chatting to Darren Emerson, lynchpin of a fledgling Underworld and, even then, a DJ of some renown. He'd been mailed a copy of '...Siren' and loved it.

He wasn't alone. Another DJ, Andy Weatherall, had also heard it and was immediately bowled over by its frenetic energy and speeded up hip hop breakbeats, so far removed from the chilly European techno he played. Weatherall was a key ally, a DJ and prime mover in dance circles who'd hooked up with Primal Scream to produce 'Loaded,' undoubtedly the ultimate indie-dance crossover hit. He'd been involved with Boy's Own from the start, writing for the fanzine that'd given the label its name and regularly playing at their parties.

At Junior Boys Own, the offshoot created when the Boy's Own name was sold on, along with doomed pop dance act One Dove, to major label London, Weatherall was constantly scouting for new records. He jumped on '...Siren' the moment he heard it, immediately persuading a delighted Ed and Tom to let him pick the record up for a full release on Junior Boys Own. Tom and Ed borrowed a clapped out old car from a friend and drove the length and breadth of the country to see Weatherall play it. "I'm sure he must have been thinking 'Those two idiots are here again," Ed reckoned.

By February 1993, the single had been given a full release, complete with interest-boosting remix from the DJ himself, who'd continually championed the record, often ending his sets with it. Immediately, on the back of Weatherall's praise, the remix offers began flooding in. For starters, they turned acid jazz bohos the Sandals' 'Open Toe' into a raging beatfest and proved '...Siren' was no fluke. They hooked up a management deal with Heavenly, the label/management/press team best known for bringing the Manic Street Preachers to the general public. DJ bookings began accumulating.

And as The Dust Brothers' star rose steadily, the Ariel situation went from bad to worse. The deal with deConstruction, with all the delays and corporate protocol that came with it, had muted the trio's enthusiasm considerably. The music industry's general apathy towards the band didn't help either. The final body blow came when the label asked The Dust Brothers to remix Ariel's single 'T-Baby.' They did it and when it never came out, the band promptly fell apart.

It was time for a break, for new things. With their courses over and 2.1 degrees under their belts, moving to London in the summer of '93 became an obvious step. The Brothers began planning the follow up to '...Siren' in between handling mixes for American rapper Justin Warfield, Bomb The Bass and Justin Robertson's

life is sweet

Lionrock outfit, ironically enough, signed to deConstruction. And starting their first weekly residency in the capital, at Soho's Job Club, usually playing so early their only audience was a member of the bar staff collecting glasses.

They took time out to rehearse a live set - vitally important to them with their indie roots - and debut at Sabresonic, Andy Weatherall's dingy but vibey weekly night at London's grimiest club, Happy Jax in London Bridge. It's a success and more gigs offers immediately fly in.

And somehow, during this first frantic outburst of activity, Tom and Ed manage to make it into their new studio in Elephant and Castle, South London, to record the '14th Century Sky' EP.

If you could ever note a watershed time in the career of the Dust Brothers, then this was it. Before '14th Century Sky,' the band were practical unknowns, favoured by a tiny proportion of London's techno elite for sure, but still struggling underdogs. But from the

moment the four track EP - and its raping, pillaging opening track 'Chemical Beats' in particular - made it out of captivity and onto the streets (February 1994, to be precise), it was clear the Brothers meant business.

Weatherall loved it, of course, and Darren Emerson began bringing his set to a climax by mixing up two copies, stretching the tune toward the fifteen minute mark. But other DJs were taking note too - The Orb's Alex Paterson even asking the pair what the record was at the Job Club, blissfully unaware that the scruffy pair were responsible for its audacious tones.

But even more importantly, the nation's bedroom DJs and techno fans suddenly wanted a piece of the action too. And no wonder. 'Chemical Beats' was just what the stuffy and stale dance scene needed to boot it out of its rut. Just as Ed and Tom's DJ sets at Naked Under Leather had sorted the wheat from the chaff, marrying obscure hip hop instrumentals to beefy techno, this record seemed to have the best of all possible worlds. Anchored to a

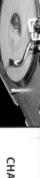

CHAPTER TWO **Siren Song**

radioactive acid line and blessed with a breakdown so outrageous it beggared belief, the tune revolved around the same hip hop breakbeats as the infant Mo'Wax stable was beginning to tout, only speeded up, pumped full of steroids and ready for the fiercest dancefloors.

The press began to take notice. Desperate for something to replace the rapidly turgifying techno that had dominated the post baggy years, they seized this electrifying combination of beats and dubbed up, tripped out sonic madness and termed it trip hop. And although it soon came to represent something quite different - the media finding it a conveniently trendy tag to sell the far more radio friendly wares of Portishead and Tricky to the public - this was a phrase that was practically invented for The Dust Brothers' 90s psychedelia. Even if, typically, they wisely avoided being typecast as trip hoppers themselves, without dodging its reflected glory.

"Chemical Beats is described as trip hop," complained Ed at the time, "but to me it's a techno record in the mould of any techno record, but it's got a chunky break on it," with Tom simply adding, "It's an acid house record." The press interest became even more frenzied with the arrival of the next EP, another tune-filled but floor-wrecking collection. 'My Mercury Mouth,' out in May that year, finally gave them the chance to build on the momentum that had been gathering slowly ever since the Junior Boys Own deal was struck. In July, they visited the US to play a rave in Orlando, Florida. Some 4,000 people turned up, principally to see the pair play a live set, shocking local promoters who hadn't sussed that 'Chemical Beats' had been such an underground hit on the other side of the Atlantic too. Afterwards, they were mobbed for autographs, something they'd have to wait a little longer for in the cooler climes of the UK.

The remix work came to a frenzied point -

always searching for the most cred-boosting names to rework their major label fodder, the big labels converged on the Dust camp demanding mixafter mix. They were only toohappy to oblige. Although remixes have come to be seen by many, in and outside the music industry, as a cynical marketing tool rather than an opportunity for creative freedom and exciting, unlikely alliances, there's no denying the importance of the medium for young producers just dipping their toes into the pool of the mainstream. Without the pressure of a release under their own names, remixes can be a rare chance for bands to relax, try out new ideas and experiment without risking their entire reputations. The pay isn't that bad either. And for those with credibility by the bucketload but little or no track record as such, it's a way of showing off versatility and scope. Without it, The Dust Brothers - who eventually gave up reworking other people's material to concentrate on their own - would have had a far slower and harder rise to fame.

Within one fortnight alone, over that summer, they completed mixes for three of their college-era heroes, The Charlatans, The Prodigy and Primal Scream. Each, cunningly enough, took their sound to fresh and very different audiences. Even then, the Dust Brothers were appearing like the common ground between so many of alternative music's disparate tribes. But it was the Scream mix that really gave Rowlands and Simons their big leg up into the treacherous waters of the mainstream. It was a classic Dust Brothers production for a start, centred around a coiling, ultra heavy breakbeat with just the sparsest touches of razor sharp guitar and a tiny snippet of Bobby Gillespie yelling "damn right!" left in. A radical overhaul of 'Jailbird' from the Scots' critically-panned second album 'Give Out But Don't Give Up,' it was everything the public had demanded from the follow up to the 'Screamadelica' but had been denied.

The band knew it too, taking the very rare step of jettisoning the original in favour of the remix on the video. The record made the Top 10 and the video, complete with Dust Brothers mix, made Top Of The Pops. The Dust Brothers had arrived.

Siren Song

CHAPTER THREE

Social Sundays

" I wouldn't really call us DJs. We're not Rocky and Diesel. We're not worthy of being mentioned in the same breath as Weatherall. We can't mix for toffee and when Tom's on the decks, instead of sorting out what's on next, I get carried away punching my arm in the air and shouting out the lyrics." Ed Simons, ID magazine, August 1994.

When the Heavenly Sunday Social first opened its doors started up on a sweaty Sunday night in July 1994, the techno community almost universally scoffed. By the end of its initial twelve week run, it had been forced to eat its words.

What it had vastly underrated was the Heavenly posse's ability to throw a party of monumental proportions. The venue, for starters, was an inspired choice. The Albany in Great Portland Street was an unpretentious, traditional English pub that had never seen the slightest slice of clubland action, never mind the calvalcade of celebrities it attracted from the start. Equally, the Social, as it was immediately nicknamed, was a welcome, down to earth refuge for stars more used to vibeless, industry-only after shows and the backbiting hordes of music biz hangers on they attracted. This, at last, was a place they could relax without the gossip mongers having a field day.

On a good night the likes of Paul Weller, Noel and Liam Gallagher, Tricky, Manic Street Preachers frontman James Dean Bradfield, Evan Dando and Bobby Gillespie would all be there, mobilised by Heavenly's ruthlessly efficient network of contacts and mates. They didn't get stared at or harassed, simply because everyone was too busy enjoying themselves to even think about it.

And in any case, everyone was equal here. It was always sold out simply on word of mouth. There was no guest list, even for the most famous faces, no queue jumping, no squeezing in after the house full signs went up, which was invariably very early. So, by 7.30pm every Sunday over that twelve week run, an amicably unruly mob of about 200 people would gather, all unsure of whether they'd even make it in. And that never did the vibe of a club any harm.

Stripping the Social of such industry hierarchies was vitally important to its success. It was a time when superclubs were at their peak, when VIP lounges to segregate glitterati from public started appearing, when admission prices were going through the roof and value for money seemed to be forgotten. The Social's almost socialist values removed it so far from soulless warehouses like London's Ministry Of Sound and Liverpool's Cream that it seemed like a revolution in itself. In fact, it was just the beginning of a far bigger upheaval that would change the face of clubland beyond recognition.

"Basically we ripped it off," Robin Turner from Heavenly would later confess to The Face, **"we ripped it off from a lot of clubs. There was Full Circle in Slough, Disco Pogo and a pub called The Swan in Windsor which was free on a Sunday night. It's a formula that works. It's for people who feel isolated by techno**

and glamorous house clubs, for people who were bored of
hearing Richie Hawtin play 'Spastik' for 20 minutes and
wanted to hear songs, have a beer and get stupid again."

If the Social's setting was inspired, its playlist was even more laced with genius. With no
quadrophonic sound systems and stadium-sized light shows to back them up, the club's
DJs were forced to rise to the occasion and pull something very special out of their record
bag. Anything less would be suicide.

The brief that Heavenly gave their vinyl spinners - play what you want, basically - was
refreshingly wide; even more so, given the fierce segregation of dance music at the time.
So a jock like David Holmes, famed for his fearsome acid techno sets, would descend the
Albany's steps with little more than a stack of Northern Soul seven inch singles to show.
Weatherall too - by this time insisting on the more serious first name Andrew - would
entertain the Social crowd with old hip hop and dub instead of the four-to-the-floor
severity he'd been roasting the Sabresonic massive with.

It was a chance for these DJs to dust off records that hadn't been touched for years or only
ever played at home, away from prying eyes and preconceptions. To surprise, entertain - to
do all the things the stuffy climes of clubland simply wouldn't allow. And the crowd reacted
wildly to it; they danced on the tables (undoubtedly impossibly uncool anywhere else) and
even on the tiny bar. They shouted along to tunes until they couldn't speak and they put
debauchery and hedonism back on the map in spectacular style.

Alcohol was consumed in vast amounts, creating a very different frenzy to the insular moodiness of Ecstasy-orientated crowds. Stories abounded of blow jobs behind the decks. And out came the amyl nitrate (poppers), the undeniably seedy but still legal drug that would eventually give its name to the whole scene. Robin Turner was regularly spotted scuttling off to Soho's porn shops - who stocked it because of its fabled ability to heighten and lengthen orgasms - to keep the club stocked up. It certainly brought back memories for Tom and Ed, who'd first encountered the drug when Most Excellent took up residence in one of Manchester's gay clubs, that sold poppers behind the bar.

Ed Simons remembers punters setting fire to numerous bottles of the highly flammable stuff then dancing in the resulting ring of flames. One time, he even had to dodge a flaming shoe hurled towards the decks by one unlucky dancer. Another's leg went up in flames after a potentially lethal spillage caught fire.And at 12 o'clock, after two hours of The Dust Brothers holding court behind the Technics, they were booted out. No dance until dawn, let the atmosphere fizzle out gradually approach here - a midnight close meant the Social was packed and buzzing from the word go to the final tune.

The Heavenly Social is centrally important to The Dust Brothers' career. Without it, they might well have made the same impact on 90s music eventually, but this was definitely their most significant launchpad to date.

They did nothing to tailor their sound to the Social's needs - they didn't need to. It was more that the Social was built to their requirements. They'd often extolled the virtues of playing smaller, spit and sawdust pub venues over the kind of glitzier clubs that Heavenly were starting to book them into. And the similarities between theSocial and Naked Under Leather - its open music policy, pub basement situation, alcoholic behaviour and general couldn't give a fuck attitude - meant they were in an ideal position to clean up.

> **"It was really exciting when it first started,"** Ed told Mixmag, **"We were playing the style we've always played, playing every week so we were able to make funny records really big records."**

The ethic of 'freestyle' - what's become the byword for snobbery-free, across the board experimentation in dance - may not have been born at the Heavenly Social, but it certainly flourished there in the capable hands of the Brothers.

They dropped Schooly D one minute and Orbital the next and capitalise on the early stages of the breakbeat revolution they'd helped kick off with 'Chemical Beats.' Trip hop of all description was beginning to filter through to the UK from America alongside more homegrown talent. Sets were frequently rounded off with communal shoutalongs to tracks so well loved no-one could resist them; Oasis' 'Live Forever' and The Beatles' 'Helter Skelter' being the most legendary, never failing to raise the roof.

And playing every week to an expectant, demanding crowd tightened up their DJing skills immeasurably. At the start of the run they were insisting they couldn't be mentioned in the same breath as Weatherall. By the end the demand for their presence in clubs across the country was outstripping booking for their mentor.

CHAPTER FOUR

In Dust We Trust

Those fabled Dust Brothers sessions at the Heavenly Social may have thrust the pair into the consciousness of the industry's elite, but they also served a much more practical purpose for Ed and Tom.

Every Sunday, alongside the pogo-friendly hip hop instrumentals and hands in the air Manic Street Preachers anthems in the pair's record box, there'd be a DAT tape or two fresh from their South London recording studio. In much the same way as drum 'n' bass producers road test their material on dubplates (specially produced one off pressings for DJing with) months before release, Tom and Ed were at last able to play new tracks of theirs that were literally only hours old.

Testing out new material in the field was absolutely vital. These were, after all, party tunes, something Tom and Ed had never made any bones about. Fucked up and distorted tunes, for sure, but still party tunes. Tracks specifically designed to make people dance - and if they didn't work at the Social, the chances were they wouldn't work anywhere else.

Dance music has always lived in big speakers, in packed rooms full of sweaty dancers. What sounds good on a pair of finely tuned studio speakers might well die on its arse in a club, where a hyped up crowd needs to be lavished with punching beats and attention-grabbing hooks almost

non-stop. Similarly, other hidden elements - some detail as apparently irrelevant as a tiny acid squiggle or a wildly oscillating hi-hit - can come from nowhere to dominate a track played at high volume, in the right environment. This was an unmissable chance for Tom and Ed to work out exactly what they needed and what they needed to dump as soon as possible. The whole of August, save their Social appearances and the odd DJing date, was devoted to recording tracks for what would become their debut album. And like all The Dust Brothers' recordings to date, the bare bones of the majority of the album was laid down in a frenzy of activity. With each track - masquerading under working titles like 'Dopeness On A Pill,' 'In Dust We Trust,' 'Just Dust,' 'Delik' and 'Just Say Yo!' - mapped out on the studio wall, Tom and Ed would spend Mondays diligently scribbling down crowd reactions and minute potential adjustments under each tune's myriad of component parts.

Strewn across the floor, one journalist from Manchester fanzine Jockey Slut who visited them mid-LP noted, were records by American rappers the Jungle Brothers, Weatherall's new band Sabres Of Paradise, old John Peel faves The Three Johns, Mudhoney, Mercury Rev, Sonic Youth and Pavement - hardly the usual dance producers' vinyl diet. Even the titles they eventually arrived at - 'Leave Home,' after a Ramones track, 'Too Many Mornings' after Bob Dylan - echoed classic rock rather than techno's obscurist sensible title dodging.

"We tend to remix rock records and indie records because there are sounds that we have no access to," Tom once pointed out, **"On dance records there aren't going to be that many sounds that we couldn't have made ourselves."**

And nowhere on the album was that indie slant more in evidence than on 'Life Is Sweet,' one of the album's two collaborations (the other being with less well known new folk chanteuse

Beth Orton). Roping in old Madchester favourite Tim Burgess of baggy icons The Charlatans to deliver the song's roaring, uplifting vocal proved to be a stroke of genius - not to mention one that would stand them in good stead for a certain other pairing with the indie world not too far in the future.

The year before they'd remixed The Charlatans' 'Patrol' single, with devastating results. "Someone gave me a copy of it when I was somewhere in Europe," enthused Burgess, "I had no idea who they were, but I thought it was amazing." But again, it was the Social - Burgess was a regular there too - that really oiled the wheels. And once the three became Sunday night drinking partners, the lush-lipped frontman was easily persuaded to visit Orinocho and contribute some vocals. A year later, they'd even been asked to return the compliment, producing a track on the Charlatans' own eponymous LP and not long after that, Burgess started DJing himself.

But for the main part, 'Exit Planet Dust' remained pure Dust Brothers, a no-nonsense introduction to their pummelling, breakbeat-heavy sound. 'Chemical Beats' was there too, still their crowning glory and by now, a flagship anthem for the pair. There were precious few surprises here, admittedly, but then they were already renowned for being an act that delivered the goods fairly and squarely, rather than messing around with new concepts and half assed stabs at the latest fashionable trend in techno. Their defence was a simple one.

"People have accused us of being formula, but that's our sound," Ed once quipped, "That's what makes us tick. It's like saying the Stone Roses album has got too many guitars on it, or Morrissey's making references to Manchester again." And for a debut album it still seemed ruthlessly dynamic and destined for a lengthy residency at the top end of the charts.

the chemical brothers

But not everyone saw it that way. At least, not at first. When Tom and Ed took 'Exit Planet Dust' to Junior Boys Own at the start of the Autumn, the label was pleased if not overwhelmed with it. Label head Steve Hall estimated it would only sell some 15,000 copies - pretty healthy for a dance record at that time, but hardly spectacular. Convinced they had a hit record on their hands, the Brothers and Heavenly management's Jeff Barratt were not best pleased. A stalemate situation was developing, and to make matters worse, the American Dust Brothers were beginning to kick up a regal stink about the unauthorised borrowing of their moniker.

Plus, money pressures were beginning to rear their ugly heads. Since moving to London, and despite keeping a hectic work schedule, Tom and Ed were still as skint as they had been as students. Tom remembers that even their acclaimed, best selling mix of Primal Scream's 'Jailbird' netted them the paltry sum of £50, as the rest of their £1,500 fee disappeared on hiring expensive valve equipment to get the sounds they wanted. They knew 'Exit...' was worth more than a limited run.

So, while lengthy negotiations went on to try and find a new home for the album, the threat of legal action against the Brothers loomed ever nearer. And after a year of building success and almost constant activity, the duo found themselves in limbo, forced to leave their future in the hands of managers and record company executives. It was to prove the most agonising delay of their career to date.

CHAPTER FIVE

Exit Planet Dust

Even now, in this gloomiest hour for The Dust Brothers, there were some compensations. Eager not to lose the momentum that recording 'Exit...' and demolishing the Heavenly Social on a weekly basis, Tom and Ed plunged themselves into sharpening up their live show.

In October 1994, The Dust Brothers were invited to join Andrew Weatherall at Liverpool's superclub Cream. Cream was a phenomenally successful club, probably the only British club ever to rival London's Ministry Of Sound in terms of reputation and consistently packed houses. It's widely been credited for single-handedly kickstarting an entire economic recovery in the city, which before it opened in 1993 was a run down and depressed place torn apart by gang violence, financial failure and drug abuse.

Cream had made its name booking the biggest house names possible - DJs like Sasha and Carl Cox were sure fire crowdpleasers and the club secured a succession of them, every Friday and Saturday night. It made business sense, and for the biggest club in North - traditionally a huge consumer of house music and before that, good time disco pop - it felt right.

chemical

And yet The Dust Brothers' visit marked a concerted effort to move away from such security, to bring their dedicated, satisfied audience something a little different. They played the club's backroom, true, but even so this remained a chance for the Brothers to prove their effectiveness in what amounted to the real world. The club's overlords, too, were looking to see whether shifting the club's agenda to more leftfield territory would work. Naturally, they and Weatherall stormed it and Cream would never be the same again - within months, the likes of Dave Clarke, jungle icon LTJ Bukem and the Brothers themselves had become regular backroom fixtures and legions of new fans were being exposed to the freshest and most exciting new music around. It was another small but symbolic step in the freestyle revolution that was enveloping Britain's electronic music scene.

Another boost to Tom and Ed's flagging morale was a commission from the world's best selling rock weekly New Music Express, for a mix tape to be given away free on the cover of the paper's Christmas issue. With a circulation tipping the 150,000 mark, the NME's double Christmas issue was always the best selling issue of the year, ensuring huge exposure for Tom and Ed. The 'Christmas Dust Up' tape, mixed at Berwick Street Studios, proved to be a tailor made showcase for their skills and eclectic taste. Opening up with their own belter 'Leave Home,' the seven track cassette at last gave them a chance to publically preview new material as well as doff their caps to their own heroes of the past. With Bonus Beats Orchestra's 'Bonus Beats' keeping up the pace after 'Leave Home,' then quickly followed up with The Prodigy's 'Voodoo People' and tracks by Depth Charge, Renegade Soundwave and Strange Brew before ending the Social-tested finale of the Manic Street Preachers' 'La Tristesse Durera,' it was a digestible distillation of those Heavenly Social sets that reached the thousands that never made it.

At last, too, they were in a position to start turning down remix offers. Dee-Lite, Fatima Mansions, Echobelly, Massive Attack and Consolidated all got the thumbs down, as Tom and Ed decided too much effort and too many ideas were being spent on remix work.

With a DJing slot on Primal Scream's Christmas tour, plus the hectic acceleration in DJ bookings that the season brought with it behind them, Tom and Ed bit the bullet and gave into pressure from the real Dust Brothers to change their name. In typically understated fashion, the replacement they chose - The Chemical Brothers, after 'Chemical Beats' - was as simple and straight forward as its predecessor, but still managed to retain that all- important hint of illegality.

And with the New Year underway things began to move on the 'Exit...' front too. Heavenly managed to secure a deal for the album to be released on Junior Boys Own, but licensed through Virgin, who'd already heard the record and shared Tom and Ed's feelings that it was a potentially huge record. In February 1995, Junior Boys Own officially licensed it to Virgin, who in turn set up their own subsidiary Freestyle Dust, exclusively for the band's work.

With things at last underway, they started preparing for the all out assault on the media and public they knew would be essential if the album was to be the success that they and Virgin believed it should be.

The live show - still fairly rare currency in dance circles in those days - was sharpening up with every one-off performance and after a triumphant support slot with The Prodigy at Brixton Academy that Spring, they soon realised this was a key asset they couldn't afford to squander.

'Leave Home' became the obvious choice for the single to precede the album, its looped refrain of "The Brothers' gonna work it out y'all" slamming the bands identity into the brains of all who heard it. It was a classic, too, a big booted bully of a breakbeat workout that matched 'Chemical Beats' in its pyrotechnic ability to bring a dancefloor to life. It wasn't until May that 'Leave Home' finally became the first Chemical Brothers record, and their major label debut to boot. It was, as it turned out, well worth the wait, as a relatively quiet singles market meant a release like this, well supported by Radio 1 and a by now sizeable fan base, could smash into the Top 20. It did, entering the singles chart at number seventeen and giving them their first bona fide hit.Confidence in the Chemicals camp was, by now, at an all-time high after the nail biting low of the past six months. All concerned were supremely confident about the album. They'd squarely rejected Virgin's suggestion they update the LP, now nearly a year old. As far as they were concerned, they were delighted with the album and that's how it would stay.

There was one last engagement to fulfil before 'Exit Planet Dust' made it in the charts. The 1995 Tribal Gathering festival, held on May Bank Holiday in Oxford, was a watershed event for British music. Veteran rave organisers Universe had held outdoor raves for years under the Tribal Gathering banner, but this year's was markedly different from its predecessors. For the first time, experienced festival-runners the Mean Fiddler organisation had teamed up with them in an attempt to expand and widen the event, which ran from the Saturday afternoon until 8am the following morning.

It was a fortuitous partnership. The Fiddler, who held a monopoly on live music venues in London, knew little about dance music but could sense that it was a rapidly mushrooming corner of the market that most promoters continually shied away from. Universe, in return, needed the financial backing and expertise in handling live bands that the Mean Fiddler's festival past afforded. Even in 1995, outdoor dance events were tarred with the brush of the original M25 raves, hopelessly haphazard and chaotic events. In the days when dance had no stars, when the event rather than any particular act was the main attraction, it didn't really matter that nobody knew who was on when and where. As house and techno had wormed their way into the mainstream, the public increasingly demanded to see their favourite acts in a well organised, value for money-delivering environment.

Even the previous year, two major outdoor techno events - the World Dance festival in Cornwall and the Lydd Air Experience, with Kraftwerk and Underworld touted as headliners - had fallen by the wayside after getting into serious financial trouble. If the general feeling was that staging an outdoor techno event in 1995 was practically impossible, that only meant the demand for such an event was bigger than ever.

Securing live sets from co-headliners The Prodigy and Orbital made Tribal Gathering a seriously attractive proposition in itself; an exhaustive collection DJs from all over the world, from Parisian techno types Laurent Garnier to big house names like Sasha, only served to make it all the more unmissable. Add an uncertainty fanned by rumours of imminent cancellation, which were circulating furiously right up until the week of the gig itself and you had enough hype and anticipation to make Tribal '95 an historical event.

It did happen, of course, and not without its problems. The weather, the downfall of many an outdoor event, was glorious, but the heat and the huge volume of traffic

chemical brothers

squeezing itself down the tiny country roads to the site at Otmoor Park, near Oxford, soon proved to be a nightmarish combination. Cars conked out left, right and centre, causing further blockages and delays. Many of the acts booked, including The Chemical Brothers, were stuck in the ensuing jam and the running order was thrown into disarray.

The chaos worked in The Brothers' favour, though. Still a relatively unknown quantity in the live arena, they'd been given a teatime slot on the main stage, which slipped back into the early part of the evening. With people finally streaming onto the site and naturally checking the activity on the main stage first, their set provided the first real energy boost of the day, with an 8,000 strong crowd greeting the new 'Exit…' material rapturously.

If the Chemicals' sound was effective in the intimate backroom of Cream and the Social's basement, it was devastating at Tribal. Like Orbital and The Prodigy, the pair had taken rave music onwards and used technology to make it all the more sophisticated, without ever losing sight of the rave dynamics guaranteed to move huge crowds.

The teasing breakdowns and tearing climaxes that tracks like 'Leave Home' and 'Chemical Beats' boasted were, quite simply, just what was needed to kick Tribal into orbit and properly launch the album in style.

Exit Planet Dust

Ed and Tom watched the rest of the evening - punctuated with DJ sets from another of their old heroes, Belgian electronic pioneer and creator of the hugely influential 'Rave Signal' tune, CJ Bolland - from a lighting tower some fifty feet above the stage. They witnessed certainly the strangest occurrence of the event, the stage invader who inexplicably began trashing The Prodigy's equipment midway through their set and forcing them to temporarily abandon the stage.

In full view of the capacity crowd he was 'dealt with' by the band and their crew before eventually scarpering backstage and escaping. It was an odd peak to what had been otherwise been a peaceful and trouble free show. But by 8am, with the sun coming up over 20,000 grinning people, it was long forgotten.

'Exit Planet Dust' finally made it into the shops the following week. The delays, it seemed, while terrifyingly frustrating for the band, had actually helped built up anticipation to the album to unprecedented levels. With the help of that key Tribal Gathering appearance, interest in the band was at a peak and the album gave the Brothers' their first Top Ten hit, shooting in at number nine.

The press, who'd been hearing most of the album in clubs and on preview tapes for most of the year, weren't quite so receptive. They didn't find too much to dissect and analyse on 'Exit...,' cautiously praising it rather than raving over its contents. Nevertheless, it continued to sell steadily, consolidated with another barnstorming live set, this time at the Phoenix Festival in Stratford in July.

This was to be the duo's only ever meeting with Megadog, the crusty techno crew who'd been largely responsible for introducing live electronic music to Britain with their all-nighters at London's Rocket club, giving acts like Orbital, Underworld and

Ultramarine the chance to play in new surroundings that combined the energy of a club PA with the space and production a full performance required. As The Chemicals were to become one of the strongest forces in live techno, it was only right they should cross paths with the Dogs. Playing alongside old mates The Orb and Underworld and with Tom, clad in AC/DC t-shirt, beginning to emerge as a larger than life, crowd-goading character, they rounded off their set with a swirling instrumental reappropriation of The Beatles' 'Tomorrow Never Knows,' a tune that would become increasingly tied up with their fate. Naturally, it brought the tent down.

So, with just this briefest pair of appearances cleverly whetting the British public's appetite for more, Heavenly dispatched an agent to book a tour of 1,000-seater venues to follow the next single, already earmarked as 'Life Is Sweet.'

"Someone said it's like turning up to work in an office job with 72 cans of lager on your desk. I think that sums it up. Our American agent said '97 is going to be massive for you' and I thought "God, if I'm doing this in two years time." Ed Simons, Mixmag, December 1995.

With months of constant graft behind them and many more months in front, Tom and Ed retired on holiday to Perpignon in France, and then, after a ten day rest, on to the dance scene's holiday haven Ibiza for a whirlwind, 24 hour DJing visit which ended in disaster when the pair were forced off the decks to "protect" them from angry Spanish clubbers who hadn't caught the Chemical beatbug quite yet. Philosophical as ever, the pair returned home amused and unperturbed, refreshed and ready for the next bout of madness that waited in store for them.

CHAPTER FIVE **Exit Planet Dust**

'**L**ife Is Sweet's' release in August offered another chance to get the Brothers' face in the papers, the added incentive of luscious, pouting Tim Burgess persuading those in the indie mainstream still unwilling to give over acres of space to what they considered to be a pair of faceless knob twiddlers, Top 10 hit album or no Top 10 hit album.

An ID caught the trio in typically disparate moods, Burgess teasing a tongue tied Tom and Ed, calling them "proper little pop stars" and adding he knew where he was with them because "one of em's hairy, the other one's fuzzy."

The eight date tour planned for the end of the summer sold out well in advance. Kicking off at Sheffield University on September 27, each show was a five hour extravaganza with DJs bookending the Brothers' set and a 2am curfew at all venues providing maximum value for money. Taking in Glasgow, Leeds, Manchester, Portsmouth Pier, Leicester and taking over Liverpool's Cream entirely for the night, the tour was already being hailed as a success before the final night at London's Astoria. Blessed with a retina-scorching lightshow by Manchester's Vegetable Vision crew, who would remain the band's visual cohorts, the show was simple but direct, Tom and Ed's heads just visible above banks of keyboards while Tom punched the air and pogoed away whenever the beats kicked in.

Tom and Ed again took the chance to surround themselves with mates old and new. Andrew Weatherall joining them at the decks on two thirds of the tour, with Justin Robertson and Cream residents James Holroyd and Paul Pleasdale filling the rest of the slots.

There was only one support band booked on the tour, and even then, only appearing at the Astoria show. Little known Parisian duo Daft Punk, who'd just released their second single 'Da Funk' on Scottish indie Soma, were just one of numerous bands beginning to follow the Brothers' through the hole they'd smashed in the wall of the mainstream. Within two years, they too would find their debut album 'Homework' landing in the Top 10. The face of music was indeed changing, with The Chemicals at the forefront.

"I can't hack going to house clubs any more," DJ Jon Carter said at the time, "Total respect to the Chemical Brothers. They came first. They've changed people's minds and opened people's minds up to it."

Carter's Monkey Mafia and Richie Fearless' Death In Vegas outfits were obvious post-Chemicals contendors, formed as they were by the next generation of DJs to grace the Heavenly Social, now relocated and revamped as a Saturday night bash at Turnmills. But there were others too; Mekon, Dirty Beatniks, Headrillaz, Supercharger and Empirion all echoed Tom and Ed's rough and ready rollercoaster approach to dance, in stark contrast to the ever smoothening sounds of trip hoppers like Mo'Wax.

A new breed of labels had also been inspired by their success; Skint Brighton and London's Wall Of Sound would become the leaders of the movement being termed big beat, as well as deConstruction's offshoot Concrete, run by Tom's girlfriend Vanessa.

And unlike lesser bands, who'd feel threatened or plagiarized by such whippersnappers, The Chemicals remained faintly flattered and certainly unperturbed. Even when Philadelphia house producer Josh Wink scored a monumental smash with his 'Higher State Of Consciousness' single, a two-time Top 10 single run through with Chemical-style breakbeats and acid touches.

"Obviously you go to record shops and you hear tracks you wouldn't have been able to hear a couple of years ago," Ed once commented, "But when we were making our records we were copying bands like Coldcut, Renegade Soundwave and Depth Charge. That's how dance music has always progressed."

The second half of 1995 turned into one endless slog of live work. There was a brief sojourn in the studio to record four of the fiercest tracks Tom and Ed had ever laid down for what would become the 'Loops Of Fury' EP. That apart, it was non-stop touring, first across Europe and then America, to build on steadily growing Stateside interest in techno. Despite inventing hip hop, acid house and techno, the three main driving forces in 90s music, the States had been desperately slow to take to dance. Britain, with its weekly music press and fast turnover of acts, has traditionally been more eager to seize on new music. And yet with grunge well dead across Europe and finally starting to decline in the States, the huge American record industry was starting to realise that it would have to find a replacement. Techno seemed to be it.

Bands like the Chemicals, Orbital, The Prodigy and Underworld had already proved - in Europe at least - that they could do everything they weren't supposed to. They could ship albums by the lorryload (The Prodigy's 'Jilted Generation' and 'Exit Planet Dust,' nearing the 60,000 sales mark by this stage, were both prime examples), play live and, most importantly of all, cross over to indie audiences.

But even with these flickering flames of interest in the music, the rigmarole of attacking the American market through coast-to-coast tours and endless meet-and-greet functions, still had to be gone through with.

Tom and Ed were beginning to feel the strain of months on the road and were itching to get back into the studio. Mixmag caught the pair at the end of their collective tether in Chicago, mid-way through the US tour, in the cover story of their December 1995 issue. "This year has been a real blur," Ed confessed, "I can't really string it together, I can't really remember what happened at all." "When we first started doing it," Ed had continued, wearily "we never thought we'd be touring or putting ourselves on the line."

The fatigue, disorientation and homesickness that life on the road inevitably causes seemed to have hit them badly, with the pair sniping at each other over their timekeeping and angrily declaring Jeff Lynne - the former Electric Light Orchestra man who'd produced The Beatles' dismal comeback record 'Free As A Bird' - as their wanker of the year.

Nevertheless the gigs, again augmented by Vegetable Vision's unrivalled visuals, were successful, with around 1000 people turning out to see them every night, respectable if not spectacular. They eventually returned home at the end of December for a badly needed recharge period, broken only by an in-store DJing session, just before Christmas at Manchester's Piccadilly Records. After the stresses and strains that 1995 had brought them, this was a final chance to relax and enjoy themselves back on their old stomping ground, doing what they'd always enjoyed best; playing records.

CHAPTER SIX

Chemical Gatherings

"   I f you've got Tim Burgess singing, why don't you get me to do a track. Only don't f-k it up or I'll chin ya." Noel Gallagher, Mixmag, November 1996.

The 'Loops Of Fury' EP, despite being a relatively low key affair simply designed to keep The Chemical Brothers in people's minds after a fairly long absence from the UK scene, came up trumps. It was a trademark Brothers production, a no-frills, fiercely dancefloor-aimed missile that received keen support from the Brothers' numerous DJ friends throughout the gig-heavy Christmas and New Year period, support which spilled over into the charts to provide the pair with their first Top 10 single. If anyone had doubted that Tom and Ed could do it on their own - the last single being the Burgess-blessed 'Life Is Sweet' - then they were proved very wrong in January 1996.

Next up was the 'Brit Hop And Amyl House (A Night In Front Of The Big Speakers)' project, compiled by Robin Turner of Heavenly and mixed by Tom. 'Brit Hop...' was the first attempt to bring the disparate house, trip hop and techno tunes heavily rotated at the Social and clubs like Big Kahuna Burger and It's On, that followed in its wake, under one collective banner. With Turner's militantly provocative sleeve notes declaring war on pseudo intelligent techno and basking in the reflected glory of the Social, its soundtrack (which included Winx's 'Higher State Of Consciousness' alongside tracks by Death In Vegas, Emmanuel Top, Lionrock as well as the Chemicals and many others) was a veritable who's who of underground sounds linked more by

attitude than style. In the resultant press coverage, the Chemicals were portrayed as the big brothers of this new, eclectic selection of brash aggro-house purveyors. Even if Ed wasn't too keen on the Amyl references; "I think it's the worst title for a record I've ever heard in my life," he said.

Tom and Ed spent the first part of 1996 getting their bearings after the eight week haul round America, laying down the foundations of the follow up to 'Exit Planet Dust' and overhauling the live set in readiness for the biggest ever Tribal Gathering yet, due to be held in May.

Originally planned for the same Otmoor Park site where 95's highly successful event had been held, Tribal Gathering '96 soon ran into problems. That Spring, in what turned out to be a highly controversial move, the local licensing authority and Thames Valley Police turned down the Mean Fiddler and Universe's application for a Public Entertainment License to hold the event, citing 95's traffic problems as their main reason for refusal. The organisers were furious and immediately appealed, claiming they'd overcome the traffic problems with a park and ride scheme and suggesting instead, that a general prejudice towards dance events was the council's real reason for refusing a licence.

The public piled in, bombarding Cherwell Valley District Council with complaints. A date was set for the appeal, to be held at a local magistrates court, only three weeks before the event. This gave the Mean Fiddler and Universe precious little leeway and when the magistrates' hearing went on for more than the two days allotted, causing another week long delay, they gave into pressure and pulled the plug.

The Chemicals, too, were angry at what they saw as an unnecessary political argument over what they saw as a well organised and important event. "Usually our live thing's a bit slapdash, but we'd actually bothered putting a new set together," Ed told Select, "We spent six weeks finishing off new stuff. If it gets rearranged we'll cancel anything else we're doing to be there."

It was quickly rearranged for a mid-June date, on a new site on the Luton Hoo Farm Estate near Luton. Tom and Ed, true to their word and anxious to air the new tracks forming in their set, immediately confirmed their appearance. As did most of the other thirty two live acts and seventy DJs, making this arguable the biggest live techno bash of all time. Underworld, forced to keep to an earlier European festival booking that clashed with the new date, were practically the only casualties.

With no Glastonbury happening during 1996, the summer became open season - and Tribal already looked like being the main event of the summer months. The Luton site proved to be a blessing in disguise - it was closer to London, for starters, but was also situated in a magically beautiful park, in stark contrast to the muddy, featureless Otmoor Park.

Headliners Black Grape, the outfit formed by indie dance icons Shaun Ryder and Bez when Madchester flagship Happy Mondays went down in early '93, were an unusual choice, but with scores of indie fans discovering the joys of electronica, it made some sense. As Ed said, "Bez is the embodiment of what Tribal Gathering will look like at 8 o'clock in the morning."

Clocking in well over an hour, the all-new Brothers set dipped further into techno territory than ever before, with a pair of new and as yet untitled tracks marking a new change in direction. "We think it's quite a lot different," Tom told fanzine Jockey Slut, "but I'm sure other people will go "Oh well, same old shit."

The combination of new, even harder material and the practice and confidence the American trip had given them, undoubtedly made their Tribal '96 show the highlight of the all-nighter, well and truly blowing a shambolic, off colour Black Grape offstage. That or the lack of artificial stimulants, possibly. "We're totally drug free," told The Face while interviewed on site, "because there were huge warning notices all over the stuff sent out saying: "Don't bring drugs on to the site. Police are searching the vans and buses." So we didn't. I'm in a drug free van now. The Chemicalless Brothers."

Chemical Gatherings

Definitely one of the strangest things about Tribal Gathering was the one persistent rumour that zipped its way around the site; that Oasis would be here and that they'd be joining The Chemical Brothers onstage. Perplexing everyone who heard it, it had no basis - there was no sign of the Gallagher Brothers throughout. However, as many a rumour monger would later be wryly conveying later that year, there is rarely smoke without fire.

Come July and the Chemicals were back on the live circuit again, playing a Phoenix Festival swamped with customers, the no-Glastonbury situation again working in its favour. With the programme enlarged to four days and The Prodigy, Underworld and Goldie also lined up for appearances in its 10,000 capacity dance tent, this was to be the Chemicals first festival headline date. They rose to the occasion, jampacking the tent on the Sunday night and leaving several thousands of people outside, simply unable to squeeze in. It was evident that next year they wouldn't be shunted off into some techno ghetto, they'd be playing the main stage.

All was going smoothly on the live front, but the Brothers were about to have their world turned upside down yet again. At the previous summer's Glastonbury festival, Tom and Ed had bumped into one Noel Gallagher backstage and reacquainted themselves with the Oasis songwriter who had, since the days of the Social, shot to interstellar success. Although Noel had been quoted on more than one occasion dismissing dance music as "just a load of bleeps," he had in actual fact, been a regular at Justin Robertson's old clubs and the Hacienda, back in the heyday of Madchester.

Backstage at Glastonbury, Noel had made a drunken offer of a collaboration - Tom and Ed had been delighted at the suggestion, but never really expected it to come off. After all, Oasis had invited the pair to spin at their after show party at their breakthrough Sheffield Arena show the year before - only to see Liam Gallagher yank them off the decks after less than half an hour, redemanding "something different...Chuck Berry or something." And the following summer Gallagher had walked into Heavenly's Soho offices and asked for a Chemical Brothers remix of 'Wonderwall,' which ended up being the band's biggest hit to date. It never became anything more than a suggestion - and there was no reason to assume that the proposed collaboration would either.

But Oasis' Creation label and Heavenly, who manage the Creation-signed act Primal Scream, have always enjoyed a close relationship, and a year later, a visit to the new Social at Turnmills prompted Noel to bring up the subject again.

Amazed and yet utterly up for it, Tom and Ed set about recording 'Setting Sun,' probably their most morphed out, complex and multi-layered composition to date. No doubt tappng into the experience they'd gained remixing Leftfield and former Sex Pistol and PIL mainman John Lydon's joint project 'Open Up,' they concocted a modern psychedelic classic with the kind of bewildering depth and sonic extremes that outstripped anything else they'd recorded.

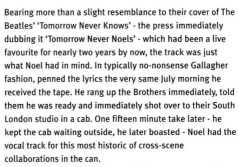

Bearing more than a slight resemblance to their cover of The Beatles' 'Tomorrow Never Knows' - the press immediately dubbing it 'Tomorrow Never Noels' - which had been a live favourite for nearly two years by now, the track was just what Noel had in mind. In typically no-nonsense Gallagher fashion, penned the lyrics the very same July morning he received the tape. He rang up the Brothers immediately, told them he was ready and immediately shot over to their South London studio in a cab. One fifteen minute take later - he kept the cab waiting outside, he later boasted - Noel had the vocal track for this most historic of cross-scene collaborations in the can.

Then the shit really hit the fan. With a huge crossover hit guaranteed, neither Creation nor Virgin were eager to relinquish their hold on the track, which would undoubtedly be one of the biggest singles of the year. Another nail biting delay ensued, bringing back memories of the 'Exit Planet Dust' rut for Tom and Ed, as the two labels squabbled for several months over the rights to 'Setting Sun.'

Eventually Creation gave in to Virgin, but at a cost. Noel wouldn't be allowed to promote the single, nor even appear in the video, despite proclaiming that the record was one of the best things he'd worked on.

Despite the business dust up, relations between the Chemicals and Oasis were further strengthened at the band's huge Knebworth shows in August. Over the two gigs held that weekend, more than 220,000 people turned out to see Oasis at what they'd claimed were the largest concerts mainline Britain had ever seen. That fact was widely disputed, but what couldn't be was the impact that Oasis had - the gigs dominated the music papers for weeks to come and a fair proportion of the tabloids too, the first time a pop band had made such waves since the 60s.

It was to be an emotional time too, as news of the death of Charlatans keyboard player Rob Collins - a close friend of both camps - had filtered through only days before the show and Noel dedicated both days' concerts to his memory.

The Chemicals had the difficult if privileged role of opening up both day's shows, with a supporting cast of Oasis' other current favourites following after; The Prodigy, Cast and Ocean Colour Scene. As well as the exposure of playing to 220,000 people, Noel's blessing was an immense boost for Tom and Ed's popularity among the indie masses. Dance music, it seems, was back on the Oasis agenda - Noel had even remixed Mo'Wax meister DJ Shadow, it emerged soon after - and for the first time, spoke about his formative years spent raving in Manchester.

"I love it really," Noel's confessed, "We had the Chemicals and Prodigy on at Knebworth. I used to go to clubs in 89 - that's how the whole Roses thing kicked off. Guys from guitar bands going to clubs. Remember that big rave Sunrise at White Waltham airfield? I got arrested there -

I think there was something wrong with the car. I used to know 808
State quite well. I did do some dance stuff in about '88 with my
producer Mike Coyle. I prefer stuff with good breakbeats. I like the
Chemicals, The Prodigy and Underworld.
"One of the things we've got is grooves - even 'Slide away,'
'Wonderwall,' the whole feel of it is highly danceable. I wouldn't say we
were a post-rave band, but we used to go to the Hacienda and then
come home and listen to The Beatles. I like both sides."

The collaboration may have raised many eyebrows within and outside the
music industry, but the parallels between the Chemicals and the
Gallaghers actually made more sense than initially thought. Tom, Ed and
Noel had propped up bars and helped fill dancefloors across Manchester
at the same, highly influential time. Then there was the Gallaghers' well
documented obsession with The Beatles, an obsession shared by the
Chemicals, who'd once declared "we're the only dance band where you get
to hear the voice of John Lennon." But the similarities went even deeper
than that; Oasis and the Brothers may have occupied very different areas
of pop culture, but their approach to making records and playing live was
stunningly similar. Both had been accused, on occasion, of peddling
formulaic fayre, for being scared of experimenting and changing their
admittedly successful blueprints. But what some people had seized on as

formula-peddling, the two bands saw as their strength - they believed what they did was essentially no-nonsense crowdpleasing that ordinary people loved. They didn't hold with the endless dissection and theorising that the music press loved to lavish on pop music, they just did what they did and did it better than anyone else.

It was October before 'Setting Sun' was released, but the fanbase support of both bands, combined with the massive interest in this apparently unlikely joining of forces, meant that it inevitably entered the charts at no1, where it stayed for two weeks. It was the pinnacle of Tom and Ed's career to date - particularly sweet for them as they'd knocked off the pale, anaemic tones of Deep Blue Something's 'Breakfast At Tiffany's,' something they took great pride in.

Noel reportedly celebrated the news at the swanky Atlantic club, washing down champagne even before the chart rundown had been announced after being tipped off by industry sources that it had reached the top spot. Tom and Ed, in contrast, gathered at Tom's house with scores of friends, all nervously listening to the new Top 40. When Deep Blue Something's irritating warblings emerged on the number two slot, the flat erupted in celebration. Even so, this was nothing over the top, just a few beers surrounded by their mates; a typically down to earth response to an out-of-this-world achievement. In any case, work on the second album was progressing fast so there was no time for hangovers.

But there was another distraction to contend with. The tabloids, desperate to get any new angle on headline grabbers Oasis, started blaming the Chemicals for troubles in the Oasis camp. To anyone who'd followed the Gallaghers career from the early days, the cancellation of their American tour that October and the non-appearance of Liam at an MTV Unplugged special filmed at Royal Festival Hall around the same time, looked like just another ruck in the long running love-hate saga of the Gallagher brothers. But to the tabloids, ignorant of the band's stormy past, it looked like the biggest band in Britain was about to split. It didn't take them long to seize upon the Noel/Chemicals collaboration, get the wrong end of the stick and start blaming Tom and Ed for the group's supposedly imminent demise. "God, we thought we were going to get lynched!" Tom remembers, "Our manager told us to keep our heads down if there were any paparazzi outside the Heavenly Social." The prospect of being confronted by hordes of militantly pro-Oasis youths at every turn didn't appeal, so they concentrated on working on the new album - with 'Dig Your Own Hole' suggested as a title - and planning another triumphant live tour.

CHAPTER SEVEN

Dig Your Own Hole

" I don't want to be in a band called the Chemical Brothers when we're 30. That is if we're still doing it together by then - we'll have to see." Ed Simons, The Face, August 1996

"All the Chemicals trademarks are here: scuffed-up breakbeats, robustly clunky electro bleeps, overheating keyboard belches, mashed-up vocal chants and sudden, jarring, head-spinning directional swerves. The difference this time is the high-speed concentration of signature tricks impacted end to end - the sound of a motorway pile-up erupting from your speakers." Stephen Dalton on 'Dig Your Own Hole,' NME, March 1997.

The politics and uncertainty of the 'Setting Sun' era behind them, the Chemicals' Autumn tour had more of the air of a lap of honour than a usual trawl round the country's venues. More than a year had passed since the last outing and the band's popularity had swelled considerably, even before the Noel team up. Last time round they'd ended the tour at London's Astoria, a modest 1,500 capacity venue - this time, they took on the capital's Brixton Academy, more than twice the size. Like the rest of the tour, most of which was conducted in venues they'd have been lucky to half-fill the year before, it was sold out weeks in advance with tickets changing hands for anything up to £40 outside.

The Brothers' old mate Justin Robertson was back on the tourbus again, too, this time fronting a live incarnation of his Lionrock outfit especially souped up and drenched in guitars for the concert circuit.

In the previous year, the set had morphed itself from a showcase for the 'Exit Planet Dust' album to something altogether. The new material now dominated their elongate, 90 minute plus show and a new generation of live classics was well on the way to establishing their presence alongside 'Chemical Beats' and 'Leave Home,' which were greeted like old friends. 'Block Rockin' Beats,' revolving around a slap-bass intro culled from 80s industrial funk types 23 Skidoo and topped off with an ancient sample lifted from Schooly D's 'Gucci Again,' was the most immediate and soon emerged as the obvious choice for the single to precede the album. They decided on 'Dig Your Own Hole' as a title, borrowing it from a piece of graffiti on the wall outside their Elephant and Castle studio. "The sheer force of someone going up to a wall and writing that," Ed said of the name, "for us it's about freedom, be what you wanna be."

If 'Block Rockin' Beats' was a heartland Chemical Brothers moment, a refinement and sharpening of the big beat aesthetics they'd continually touted to date, there were other new offerings that showed Tom and Ed were capable of more than simply rolling out the big drums and hoping for the best. Most notably, there were forays into pure techno territory - uncharted waters for the band to date - that echoed the pair's recent rediscovery of old hero Joey Beltram's work, as well as their enthusiasm for the work of the fast rising Daft Punk.

Taking up residency again at the relocated Heavenly Social at Turnmills, now a Saturday night weekly climax rather than Sunday's final blast, that Winter they roadtested 'Dig Your Own Hole's more dancefloor-friendly moments on dubplate, exactly as they'd tested 'Exit Planet Dust' in 1994. The bigger, even beerier surroundings of Turnmills proved even more of a mean testing ground than the Albany and many of the final adjustments to the album were made as a result of playing them out, which remained as essential a practise as ever.

As work on the LP neared completion at the end of '97, it was clear that the second album wasn't simply going to be a rerun of 'Exit....' The press, while showing grudging admiration of their successes, had continually panned the pair for the supposedly formulaic nature of 'Exit...' and the 'Loops Of Fury' EP. They were about to be proved wrong.

Tom and Ed had lined a number of collaborations for the LP that would again showcase the wide vision and taste essential to making interesting, long lasting records. The album would, of course, contain 'Setting Sun' - in a new, elongated version - but they'd again drafted in Beth Orton to provide the vocals for the LP's only other fully fledged song 'Where Do I Begin.' Segs, bassist of pub rock punks The Ruts, added his bass to 'Lost In The K-Hole' and American weirdrockers Mercury Rev, who'd long shared their vision of psychedelic headf-k music, provided them with a DAT full of clarinets and sonic strangeness and told them to do their worst. The end result was to be the album's final track 'The Private Psychedelic Reel,' one of the most original productions to date, prompting Ed to comment "It's really moving, really makes your heart explode."

With the album in the can, '97 looked like the year The Chemicals would take over. The underground was bursting with Chemical-inspired contendors, the radio couldn't get enough of their singles and they'd already been asked to play live at Glastonbury for the first time. European festival bookings were also flooding in.

Tom and Ed crowned off their best year yet at another Universe/Tribal Gathering function, their whopping 10,000 capacity rave at Alexandra Palace on New Years Eve. Centred around a live performance from Orbital, who'd also enjoyed their most triumphant year yet with several Top 10 singles, the Chemicals were initially approached to play live, but with all the attendant hassles that came with the territory, opting instead to DJ in one of the smaller rooms.

The gig was a sell out, naturally, and the room the Chemicals were due to play in was swamped with punters hours before they were set to play. Fearing a crush, security closed off the room, meaning hundreds of Tom and Ed's fans who'd paid more than £20 to get into the Mount Universe event, were unable to see them. It was an unfortunate end to the year, but it failed to dampen their spirits.

CHAPTER EIGHT

Block Rockin' On

" **W**e had such a good year last year as far as having fun goes and I think 1997 has got a real optimistic happy vibe to it already. I've just been driving around listening to the music on Radio One and it just seems so different, really good. Hopefully, the days of listening to dreary old Gene are drifting into the past." Ed Simons, NME, January 1997.

"Do your sounds taste of anything? Can you smell them?"
Newsweek journalist quizzing Tom and Ed in America, 1997.

If Britain, suddenly seizing alternative culture in general and techno in particular to its breast after Britpop's conservative retro overkill, seemed like a new country when 1997 dawned, America was about to undergo an even more dramatic change.

The Chemicals were no virgins when it came to the States. After all, they'd been received warmly over there before anyone beyond their immediate family of supportive DJs and friends was even vaguely interested. But when they visited the USA early on in '97, even they noticed that there'd been a sea change in opinion towards techno.

There was MTV, that all important arbiter of taste that decided more than anything, what would sink and what would swim in the US mainstream. Dominated by rock, hip hop and R&B in the States for years, it'd had suddenly grasped techno as a replacement for the ailing grunge scene,

chemicals

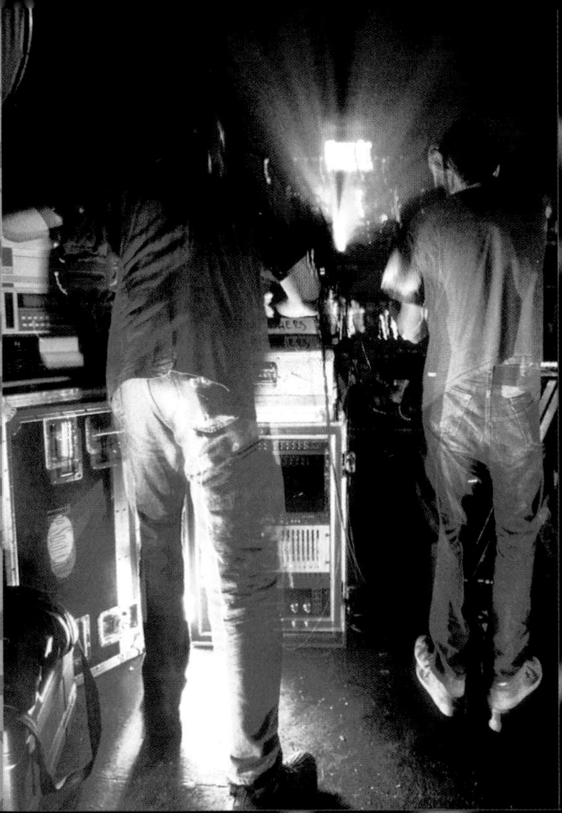

launching a prime time dance show Amp and programming more and more electronic music into their schedules. It was even running news programmes explaining this apparently 'new' musical revolution to its viewers - despite the fact the Yanks had invented the stuff!

There was also much encouragement to be had in the Stateside victories of the Chemicals' contemporaries. Not long back, The Prodigy had been the hottest British property going, prompting a 20-label bidding war to snap them up which ended with Madonna's Maverick imprint shelling out a reputed £3 million to secure their services. Stadium giants U2 invited them to join their enormodome 'Pop' tour but they turned the offer down, determined to make it alone.

The smaller end of the States' live circuit had opened up to the delights of The Orb, Underworld and Orbital too - "Every time we'd been there in the past," said Orbital's Paul Hartnoll of their end of '96 American tour, "the only way promoters would deal with it was if it was some travelling rave affair. Everyone always said that to play America you had to get the ravers along and have a rave, but that's just complete bullshit, because Americans don't seem to be like that any more."

Talk of a huge, British-invasion rave on Independence Day at New York's Madison Square Gardens began emerging as soon as '97 started, as potent a symbol of techno's long awaited arrival as anything.

As well as their regular visits to the other side of Atlantic, The Chemicals had at least one other advantage over the rest of the competition - Noel Gallagher. While Oasis hadn't quite been able to emulate the scale of their phenomenal British success, they were still doing well in the US, with their 'What's The Story (Morning Glory)' album taking up a fairly permanent residence in the US Top 40. The added kudos of Noel's vocals on 'Setting Sun' (sales of which in Britain had steamrollered their way up to 300,000) meant the single straight away shot into the lower end of the relatively impenetrable Billboard 100.

"The Prodigy seem to be getting all the attention," moaned Ed at the time, "but we've already done three big tours out there, filling venues bigger than them a long time ago. We really love playing in America. It's like 1989 for them, all pretty new and it's refreshing." It's was true - 'Exit Planet Dust' had already shifted 150,000 copies Stateside.

MTV, too, who started playing the video for 'Setting Sun' that Spring and had treated it to heavy playlist rotation ever since, stepped up their interest. On a five day promotional visit funded by their American label Astralwerks - home to Future Sound Of London as well as a host of smaller, more credible acts like µ-Ziq and Space Time Continuum - they were interviewed by the station's 'Alternative Nation' show.

Conducted in a downtown restaurant, the interview was an amusingly typical Brothers' encounter, the band responding in a bemused fashion to interviewer Kennedy Montgomery's increasing excited questions. Tom and Ed may have been declared "Techno's first rock stars" by the American press, but their interview manner remained a million miles from the hard sell, personality plus approach of that rock bands grow up on.

Never ones to be cajoled into making fools of themselves for the mere sake of making entertaining viewing, the Brothers' lack of verbosity has long been confused with a lack of personality on their part. Wrongly so - they're just far happier to let their music do the talking.

Take Ed's explanation of 'Dig Your Own Hole' - **"I think it's commercial 'cos it's an hour of really quite pleasurable listening. I just thing it's a really good soundtrack for people living today."** No gratuitous slagging off of their contemporaries, no larged up arrogance and certainly no pretentious theorising.

And that, ultimately, is what people appreciate about The Chemical Brothers. Their music remains as scratchy and rough as a bedroom techno prodigy's first cut and paste effort, regardless of success. They are two ordinary people in a world filled with inflated egos, all desperate to sell their souls for fame. Tom and Ed aren't - if you like what they do, fine, if you don't, tough. You want attitude? Listen to the records - there's plenty enough there to go round.

They returned refreshed, eager to get 'Dig...' to the public and get out on the road yet again. Another UK outing was secured for the Spring of '97 - and another Brixton Academy sell out assured - with Richie Fearless' Death In Vegas supporting. Legendary New York hip hop DJs Kool Herc and Grand Wizard Theodore - the original old skool rap heroes - were added to the bill for the London date, reflecting the fact that as well as the teeth grinding techno of Joey Beltram, the pair had rediscovered 80s hip hop of Afrika Bambaataa and his cohorts in a big way.

Always looking forward and unhappy to retread already trodden ground, Tom and Ed promised new changes to their live show. Tom might even get out his guitar, Ed threatened, letting slip that Tom's six string pluckings had already made it onto countless Chemicals releases, only so warped and distorted by technology that no-one had noticed.

'Block Rockin' Beats' came out in mid-March. Backed with a video that - shock, horror - actually featured a three second cameo role from Tom and Ed, it gave them their first 'proper' number one. Any comments suggesting they couldn't do it without the help of a sizeable star like Noel Gallagher was instantly silenced. A stream of magazine front covers, from heartland indie rag Select to ultra cool style bible The Face, plastered their faces across the newsstands.

The Face interview stood out among the morass of press around the time and not only because the attendant photo session inexplicably portrayed an uncomfortable looking Tom and Ed dressed in top hats and tails, their eyes touched up to look like demon's. During the interview, Face writer Sylvia Patterson played the band a selection of would-be big beat classics and asked them for their opinion. It was rare opportunity to elicit some honest held, controversial opinions from the Chemicals, a band usually loathed to criticise anyone. They declared U2's Chemically beated stab 'Mofo' - part of their dance-tinged 'Pop' LP and another sign of the Brothers' huge influence on mainstream pop - was "Undignified, frankly" and Wall Of Sound's biggest selling act Propellerheads "uninspiring." And of Dutch breakbeat merchant Eboman, Ed confessed "Probably one of the major inspirations on our album is this sort of record making us go "no more."

Skint's Bentley Rhythm Ace crew and The Prodigy got the thumbs up, however, as did Primal Scream's comeback single 'Kowalski,' of which Ed said "Don't think they've been listening to a lot of Chemical Brothers records. They've been holed up with our drum machine, though. 'Cause they borrowed it." Tom simply added the ultra-dry "So that's a very direct influence."

The piece also managed to weedle the pair's most direct statement of intent to date. "We're not trying to change the world particularly," Ed stated bluntly, "what we do is not that important. Even though we take it very seriously. It's just about people having a good time and *weeeell*, I suppose that's revolutionary - it's a good life force to have, that every Saturday night you're involved in someone's night out. So yeah, it's a celebration. And I think you can hear that on the records."

With acclaim and unequivocal praise finally coming their way and 'Block Rockin' Beats' soundtracking Saturday nights everywhere from superclubs to student unions, it looked as though the Chemical Brothers had finally achieved the impossible. They'd dragged dance out of its trainspotter-inhabited ghetto and made it the universal, classless force it was when acid house first kicked off at the end of the 80s.

It now seemed inconceivable that 'Dig Your Own Hole' would fail to follow 'Block...' to number one. America beckoned, arms open and Europe still couldn't get enough of their block rocking beats. The hole in British music the Chemicals were about to dig was bigger than they'd ever anticipated - and the story was still only really beginning to take shape.